Comments from some of Marilyn's clients:

"Bless you, Marilyn! You have succeeded in making this as easy as possible for me. It could have taken me years to come up with this kind of detailed plan, with so much taken into account! Truly, this has saved a lot of time and frustration, I'm certain. I feel so much gratitude and relief for this kind of support from you...wow."

Barbara Larson
Bainbridge Island, Washington

"You helped me get off my you know what and get something done that was very important to me. I needed a partner I could trust, who had the skills to help me. Thank you for your support and encouragement."

Barbara Urschel
Orcas Island, Washington

"Using Marilyn's system, I never feel at loose ends. I no longer feel that I'm spending my valuable time getting organized, because I stay organized! When my desk and office become cluttered, I simply start dispersing items to the appropriate spot, or create a new spot and presto—I'm ready to work! Thank you, Marilyn!"

Rhonda Barnett, Senior Sales Director
Mary Kay Cosmetics, San Diego, California

"I learned not to forget about what I love doing, and include it as part of my day in order to stay motivated."

Maria Contreras
San Diego, California

Also by Marilyn McLeod:

Conscious Networking
Finding and Creating Your Ideal Communities

Peer Coaching Reference
Extending Your Coaching Dollar

Recession or Plenty
7 Steps to Success in Business & in Life

Secrets of Self Publishing
Digital Tools for Publishing and Marketing

Social Media Series:

Social Media for Beginners
Step by Step for Small Business

Social Media for Small Business
Tips for Using Your Time Effectively

How to Work with Your Web Developer
Asking the Right Questions

Social Media Strategy
Navigating the New World Online

Social Media Workbook
Creating Your Master Plan

Social Media for Small Business

Tips for Using Your Time Effectively

by Marilyn McLeod

Consider the Possibility Press
www.considerthepossibilitypress.com

Social Media for Small Business
Tips for Using Your Time Effectively

For information:

Consider the Possibility Press
http://www.considerthepossibilitypress.com
P O Box 703
Cardiff-by-the-Sea, CA 92007 U.S.A.
+1-760-644-2284

Library of Congress Catalog Card Number

International Standard Book Number
9780982229019

Printed in the United States of America

Social Media for Small Business
Tips for Using Your Time Effectively

This book is written for busy small business owners who have little cash and even less time.

Quickest route to something usable in this book:
Chapter 2 "10 Minute Tasks" (page 9)

The social media landscape changes very quickly. Some content in this book may change by the time you read this. To keep up with changes look for future editions of this book. You may also follow me on Twitter @marilynmcleod and find the social media book series Facebook fan page via www.CoachMarilyn.com.

I hope this book helps you become more relaxed about your schedule, and that you are able to enjoy your social media experience even more, and be more effective as a result.

Join me online as we learn more together!

Marilyn McLeod
San Diego 2010

www.CoachMarilyn.com

Introduction

For some reason, time management and organization have always been natural for me. Because of this I've been able to translate complex tasks into step by step processes others can follow and use to shorten their learning curve and optimize use of their resources.

As a small business you don't have to spend as much time as large corporations going through committees and boards in order to get your social media budget funded. You can just schedule ten minutes or an hour in your calendar and try a few things to see how they work for you.

The administrative burden social media can place on the already overflowing plate of a small business owner can seem onerous … how in the world can you add one more thing, even it is important? This may seem an especially valid question if you already don't look forward to sitting at your desk to handle email each day.

Because you're probably more focused on your craft, on your subject matter, than how to navigate the online world, you may simply want to hand off this task to someone else. In this book I provide guidelines in terms of what you can hand off, and what makes most sense to take care of personally. Hopefully the social media tools and your ability to manage your time will decrease your burden in other administrative areas.

If you need more support, check my website for seminars, teleclasses and coaching opportunities.

Marilyn
www.CoachMarilyn.com.

About the Author

Marilyn McLeod has been working with organization and time management concepts throughout her career, at times teaching time management courses and often providing individual coaching for small business owners.

Her quest for efficiency led her online in 1996 where she began to provide online resources to her coaching clients.

Soon other small business owners asked her to help them with their online presence, and today she is translating the large world of social media into bite-size pieces for people at all levels of online expertise.

Join her in this book to learn more about how to organize your schedule and your social media efforts to make best use of your precious time.

You can find more about Marilyn at her online hub: www.CoachMarilyn.com

Table of Contents

CHAPTER 1

Social Media – Simply a Time Drain?

ℰℭ

As a small business, you're especially close to the bottom line so you're always trying to do more with less. I know you want to get more marketing exposure with fewer ad dollars. I know you also want more results with less effort because you're already too busy. The promise of social media is free advertising to reach an unlimited audience. The cost in dollars is usually free or very low. The cost comes in as time invested. I'm writing this book to help you use your limited time in the most effective way to support your business and personal goals.

This is a very social environment. As a small business it's easier for you to blend into the social media world because it's really about individual people. The culture is casual and personal. It's about being authentic, humble, relevant and helpful. Large corporations often have a social media presence, but it's about their brand. They have individuals posting for them, which is useful and often very effective, but as a small business or entrepreneur your business is probably closely associated with you as an individual, so social media is a more natural fit.

What makes social media so effective is it's set up to be viral. It's communication and integration on steroids. If your followers or friends or connections like what you've sent them and think it'll help their network, they'll pass it along, giving you credit (at least that's the overall culture of the social media world). You provide valuable content that people want and this naturally creates awareness for you and your business model.

People want to be heard. If you respond to them with interest and appreciation, it shows them they've been heard, and they'll want to give back to you.

Social media doesn't replace how you're already promoting, unless what you're doing now isn't getting you anywhere and you decide to try social media instead. Keep up your marketing efforts that are working, and use online marketing and social media to support your marketing message.

Social media gives the customer control. It's about attracting your ideal audience to you. It allows you to inform them and it allows you to get insights from them. It's a two-way conversation. You can even eavesdrop on many conversations that are public. Find people that match what you're looking for and begin interacting with them. Join in their conversations when you have something to offer.

Because your social media efforts allow you to keep your name and information in front of more people each time you post a new message and possibly long after, social media can help you retain people in your network. You can energize a certain number of them to take action. You can find new people to add to your network. Your contributions and presence can enhance your reputation as a reliable authority in your niche and help establish your brand based on your expertise.

If you're using it to socialize rather than promote your product, how do you make money with social media? Think about how you make money offline. How do you gain new customers? You probably cultivate new relationships, find a way to help those people, build trust and rapport, and finally, if there's a match and you're there when they need what you offer, you may have a new client.

You can reverse the client chase! As you present yourself and make connections and friends online, you show them how to find your online home base so they can get to know you better. You can then lead them to your offerings and give them a clear way to respond and ask for what you offer. If you hear back any comments that sound critical, open your heart, be authentically curious, and reflect on the need behind their comment. They've just given you their consulting services for free. Look for the nugget behind the style of their message for how you might tweak what you do to become even more unique and valuable in your field (see Chapter 6 "Universal Needs Chart", page 59).

Social media certainly can be a time drain, especially if you allow yourself to spend endless hours in conversation. You could have a team of people working full time implementing the possibilities I list in this book and still not use everything to its fullest extent, so don't worry about getting it all done. Just do what you can. Make strategic choices about how you spend your precious time, and be conscious of your actual time spent day to day.

In an article in Business Week (March 10, 2009), David Allen discusses "Time Management in the Age of Social Media". He recommends targeting your social media very closely to attain your goals, rather than '... indiscriminately hook into multiple sources of poorly defined static. To use social media effectively, just be sure that you aren't putting more effort in than the result you're getting.'

We've evolved to a very complicated Internet-scape where it's easy to get lost and overwhelmed, yet at the same time it's difficult to hide. Since our personal lives to some extent have gone public, we might as well have a voice in how we're perceived.

The game is changing. What happens when artists start selling their downloads directly from their own pages instead of using the big labels? Why share the revenue when they can go directly to their customers?

There are direct ways to monetize your online presence, but even if you don't have a call to action on your blog or website that leads to an order form, your online efforts can still contribute to income. As your network grows and people know what you stand for and become familiar with your message, you may receive invitations to speak at conferences and contribute to articles and books, and may be quoted in the media, all of which will help you grow your list. If you're clear about what you do and what you want, eventually you'll find yourself attracting prospects and buyers. The larger and more finely tuned your network, the better results you'll receive when you send out a post to your network.

Are you having a tough time trying to quantify or forecast what the benefits will be of investing in social media? It's true; it's not immediately measurable. The cost of building your business using social media is your time. Decide how much time you'll put in, or how much money you'll spend on someone to help you (see Chapter 5 "Automating and Delegating", page 39). Evaluate the traffic that comes into your hub and look at sales. If you're not getting enough results after a week or so, adjust what you're doing to improve the outcome.

How do you know what's real and what's not when you read something online? Think of how you discern truth in other areas of your life, when you read something in the paper, hear a story on television, or listen to a neighbor passing along a story about someone else. Is it true or not? If you try to have the best people in your network, and you hear the same thing from more than one person who all have a track record of seeing the truth, maybe there's something to it.

Each social media site has its own culture and its own rules. Become acquainted with both, and follow their lead as you introduce yourself on their site and interact with their members. Keep your standards high when you post on these sites. Come from a place of sincerely wanting to help other members. Think before you post. Post when you have something of value to contribute.

If you're just leaving a party where you've had too much to drink and you feel compelled to send a tweet, don't. If you're angry or upset about something, wait until you've calmed down and can be clear about what you really want. Then make a clear request that will help you get what you want. Tweets and posts last. Think of how you want to be seen in the future before you hit the 'send' button. Is this something memorable and of value? Is it something you'll be proud of in the future?

How to Protect Yourself from Overwhelm

Whenever you get that feeling that it's just too much, stop whatever you're doing and allow a deep breath. Whew! The world sure is full of wonderful options and possibilities, isn't it?! My friend Marshall Goldsmith talks about 'drowning in a sea of opportunity'. It happens to all of us.

Sometimes this feeling of overwhelm is an indication we're moving into a territory we don't immediately see as aligned with our goals, and it's our inner voice trying to get our attention that we've gone off track. Or maybe we've been working for six hours straight, our blood sugar is getting low and we need some good protein and nutrition … or just a glass of water! Our brains work much better when we're hydrated. Or maybe we're scared because we don't have some bit of information or the skills to take our project to the next step.

Instead of walking away in frustration, take a quiet moment to go a little deeper into your thoughts or feelings to see what might be behind that feeling of overwhelm. If you're hungry but still on a deadline, write down two unanswered questions you're working on and carry them with you to dinner. Don't beat yourself up trying to push the answers out of yourself. Really make your dinner hour peaceful and enjoyable, and just have the paper with unanswered questions handy so you can look at it when you've rested and your mind starts naturally becoming interested again. Remember … you're on a one-hour vacation! You can work if you want, but only if you want. Just for this one hour. Or ten minutes. Whatever you can afford time-wise.

If you're getting off track, figure out where you left the main road and go back there to start. If you've gone off on a wonderful tangent and developed ideas and information you might use later, document what you've learned so far and put it in a folder for later reference. Then focus again on the main track to complete your immediate task.

If you realize you don't have enough information or the right skills to complete the next step, think about how you might get the information, how you might acquire the skills, or who might be able to help you.

If you're simply exhausted and want off the treadmill, finish whatever you need to accomplish immediately (if anything) and then schedule some time off where you really have no responsibilities except to yourself. Go through "Time Management Applied" (page 15) or "Values to Daily Tasks" (page 35) and revisit your choices. We all have to work to make ends meet, and sometimes do things when we'd prefer to play or do work that's more interesting, but there's a limit to how much we can push ourselves. Our bodies or relationships will suffer at some point if we don't take care of our basic needs.

Think about your basic needs. Turn to "Universal Needs Chart" (page 59) and do a few exercises. Identify your own basic needs at this point and make plans to meet them within your current frame of reference.

Summary

- Most aspects of social media are free; your investment is time.

- The culture is casual and personal, and it's more about individuals than organizations.

- Authenticity, humility and a sincere effort to be helpful are the currency of the culture.

- Social media is so effective because it's set up to be viral.

- People want to be heard. Respond to them with sincere interest and appreciation.

- Social media gives the customer control.

CHAPTER 2

10 Minute Tasks

ℰↄ

In this chapter I'm going to assume you grabbed my book on the way out the door, you've turned to this chapter after sitting down on the train and you've got twenty minutes to read the paper and do something to make progress on your social media campaign. I'll just take up ten minutes so you have the other ten to catch up on the news.

10 MINUTE TASK 1:
What's New for Your Audience

While you're reading the paper, make notes about news your target audience will appreciate. If you've got an Internet connection and you're reading online, note the url of the story so you can link to it later. For now write a 120-character-or-less message about the news item. It should be compelling, provocative or fun in some way, and if possible, include some of your key search terms.

10 MINUTE TASK 2:
What to Do With This Message When You Get to the Office

Go to a url shortener like www.bit.ly. Paste in the long url and click the button to get a shortened version. Copy the shortened version to the end of your 120-character-or-less message, then go to your Twitter account and send your post! If you don't yet have a Twitter account, go to 10 Minute Task 3!

Twitter

10 MINUTE TASK 3:
Create a Twitter Account

Go to www.Twitter.com and create an account. Be sure to use an email address you check often, and come up with a Twitter handle (username) that supports you either personally or supports your brand or product line, depending on how you plan to use that Twitter account and the image you want to project online.

10 MINUTE TASK 4:
Check the News on Twitter

Go to search.twitter.com and look at trending topics to see what the Twitterverse is thinking at the moment. Then type in some key search terms ... your company name, your @twitterhandle, your key competitor's name, key topics in your field. You're searching real-time conversations that are either happening right now, or that happened very recently.

10 MINUTE TASK 5:
Responding to the Conversation

If you're doing your Twitter search and you see an interesting message that you have an urge to respond to, go ahead and do it! If you find people have mentioned your @twitterhandle or retweeted something you posted earlier, send a public message thanking them for the mention or the retweet. Be sure to include their @twitterhandle (for example @marilynmcleod) in your message as you thank them.

LinkedIn

10 MINUTE TASK 6:
Create a LinkedIn Account

Go to www.LinkedIn.com and create a new account. Be sure to use your real name and a personal email address you check often. Don't get fancy just yet ... put your real first name and last name in the appropriate boxes. Put in your current position, and here you can get a little fancy ... use the title box to describe what you do, using your key search phrases in the description.

10 MINUTE TASK 7:
LinkedIn Answers

Log into your LinkedIn account and look at the Answers section. Search by your key search terms, and see if there are any questions you can answer.

10 MINUTE TASK 8:
Network Update

Send a Network Update letting people connected with you on LinkedIn know what you're up to. Say something that's informative and useful to people reading your mini-post, and something that highlights what you do. Use key search terms as appropriate.

Blog

10 MINUTE TASK 9:
Ideas

As you're talking with customers or your target audience during the day or exchanging emails, write down the kinds of questions they're asking and the topics that come up in conversation. Keep a notepad of these topics and questions along with your response. This will be very helpful later for writing blog posts.

10 MINUTE TASK 10:
Repurposing Content

As you record your ideas for future blog posts, also jot down related messages in 120 characters or fewer which you can use later for tweets in Twitter.

Strategy

10 MINUTE TASK 11:
Seasons and Cycles

Take a piece of paper and write on separate lines each month of the year, January through December, so you have twelve lines with a space between each line. Now think about what you're usually doing each month, what your company is doing, and what your customers are doing and thinking about. Use this later as you're planning when to publish blog posts.

10 Minute Task 12:
Focus

Periodically review your progress and plans as compared with your mission, your goals, your purpose. Make adjustments so everything aligns strategically with what you're trying to accomplish in your larger picture.

Summary

- If you can schedule a regular time to check the social media accounts you've set up, it'll keep you in the flow of conversation and you'll be in a better position to make meaningful connections with the people in your social network.

- This time might be ten minutes here and there where you can find it in your day.

- After a time you'll discover which social media activities give you the best results, and you can develop your own list of '10 Minute Tasks' that fit your goals, your schedule, and your approach to social media.

CHAPTER 3

Time Management Applied

ℰᴒ

Do you find yourself getting lost in your online experience, perhaps finally 'coming to' about 3am and then dragging yourself through the following day?

Do you find yourself avoiding the whole computer or social media thing because you just don't have time?

Alright, I admit it! The length of this time management chapter may not give you the sense it's going to help you have more time. Just reading it alone will take some time, and answering the questions and following through on the tasks ... even more time. But you probably picked up this book because you wanted to improve something about how you use your time and I want to give you a complete guide. Take the sections that can help you now and leave the rest. I don't apply all of them myself all of the time. If this isn't an issue or you don't have time to go into depth right now, go ahead and skip this chapter.

I suggest it might be worthwhile in the long run to schedule a day, or a series of part-days, to go through this chapter point by point. What I hope you'll get as a return on your time investment: happier, more productive days, more clearly focused on what really matters to you, and less focused on giving away your precious resources to things that either don't really matter to you, or may be outdated, or don't really matter to the project or the person you're doing the work for. How great would that be?!

How successful do you feel in general in terms of using your time effectively? Do you depend on a system to keep you on track throughout the day, or do you just go out there and wing it?

I don't have any judgments about strategies ... it's really about whatever works best for you. If you're keeping track of commitments and following through so your customers feel happy with their deliverables, and you're making progress toward your goals and enjoying your day ... as far as I'm concerned, you're there!!!

Personally I find I'm more effective when I have clarity. The more unknowns, especially about which next steps I expect of myself, the less I'm able to focus my resources effectively and the more I find myself staring into space or engaged in what may seem like useless activities. Sometimes a 'useless' activity actually gets me off the treadmill long enough to mentally process experiences of the day and is highly valuable, and sometimes it just uses up my valuable time.

If you would like to make some improvements in your time management habits, following are ideas for your consideration. For more information check out my book *Recession or Plenty: 7 Steps to Success in Business & in Life*.

Clear Your Work Area

Expectations

Let's start by pulling everything out of your pockets, purse, wallet, desk, and all the mental lists you carry around without writing them down. Let's get it all on the table and see the size and breadth of the burden you've been carrying.

There have been times in my life I specifically decided not to do this because I knew the real list was far more than I could begin to deal with, and if I put it where I could see it all I would feel so overwhelmed I wouldn't be able to accomplish anything. That may be true for you, or not. You don't have to do it all at once. There may be many things you're carrying around with you that you don't have to do at all. You won't know if you don't look. If you feel so moved, be brave and at least take a peek. If you prefer, start by making a list of just the surface items you're dealing with this week, or today.

If you're comfortable using Excel, it's an excellent tool for this work. You can also follow this process with pen and paper. I'll give the instructions as though you're using Excel.

> **In this book when I give instructions on how to navigate a software program, I'll put the instructions in brackets [ ].**

Make a List

Open Microsoft Excel and create a new document [File, New] and save it [File, Save As] to the RESOURCES folder on your computer. Call the document To Do, or something similar.

Create the following column headings: Status, Priority, Purpose, Value, For, Type, Description, Comments [click in the table cell at the very top left at the coordinates A1 and begin typing, then tab to the next cell, and so on].

Make a list of everything you can think of you're responsible to carry out, listing the items in the Description column [if you click in the first cell under Description and type the item, you can usually press Enter to get to the next cell down]. If it's helpful, add information in the Comments column if you need more room. Go back and add a word in the Type column for each item. Type might be: email, call, visit, research, etc.

Next add a word in the For column. This will probably be a person's name: your boss, a family member, yourself, etc.

Now add a word in the Purpose column for each item. Purpose would either be the name of a project, a word describing the reason you're taking on this responsibility, etc.

Just off the top of your head (we'll revisit this later), go through and put in a Priority: A, B, C, etc.

Status you can use now or later: How far along is this item in terms of completion? Add a word or code to help you remember.

Values: This column will be useful after you've completed the exercises in Chapter 4 "Values to Daily Tasks".

You can add more columns to the spreadsheet later if this helps you track your work.

Well, there it is! All in black and white, all in a row. Did you know you were carrying that much around in your head? There are benefits to using systems like this, for instance you now have more room mentally to think about other things instead of using your impressive mental abilities to remember to pick up milk or write your speech for the next conference. You can schedule a time

18

to pick up milk or write your speech, and think about it the day it appears on your schedule.

Another benefit is that putting it all out on the table gives you a chance to look at it objectively as a whole. I find it's very helpful to have the list in Excel.

Use Excel to Track the Details

How to Sort in Excel:

Click on the upper left corner of the spreadsheet, so it selects the entire worksheet.

[Data, Sort]

Look at the bottom of the dialog box first: My list has ... be sure to check [Header row].

Now you'll be able to sort by column headings. You have several search options; just use the ones that are useful.

How to Print Your List

Sometimes you may want to print your list, or only a portion of your list. A helpful technique first:

[File, Page Setup]

Page tab: Choose [Portrait or Landscape], depending on how much you want to see on each page, or how you want to view the list.

Margins tab: I suggest you keep the top margin the way it is, to make room for the page header. You can adjust other margins if you want, for instance, to make the left margin wider to make room for punching holes.

Header/Footer tab: This is a great tab. You can click on [Custom Header] and type what you want to see as the name of this document (I usually put this in the middle, where it's centered, in larger type), and page numbering (I usually put this on the right … just click on the button marked [#], and put the word 'page' in front if you want). Then click OK.

Sheet tab: This is also an important tab. You can choose whether or not to have [gridlines] (I find them very helpful). Click in the white input box next to [Rows to repeat at top]. Then click on your actual Excel document in the 1 so it selects the row with your column headings. This puts $1:$1 into the white input box, and also prints the right column headings on each page.

Click OK.

How to print everything:

[File, Print]

Print range: [All]

Print what: [Active Sheet]

How to print only selected columns:

To print everything in certain columns: Click once at the very top of the columns you want to print, above your column headings where it says A, B, C, etc., so these columns are highlighted to show they're selected. Hold down the [Ctrl] key while clicking to select more than one column.

To print a few items that are adjacent to each other: Click in the upper left cell you want to print, and drag the cursor to the bottom right cell you want to print.

Either way, after you've highlighted the areas of your spreadsheet you want to print, here's how to print just that much:

[File, Print]

Make sure Print what says [Selection]

Click [OK]

How to Analyze the List

You can sort by various columns, for instance, by the For column. How does the For column match with the Priority column? Is there someone in your life who's taking up most of your time and resources? Do you agree with this allocation of your resources? If not, is there something you can do to rebalance?

You can also sort by Type, which helps you pre-schedule time to do all of your emails at once, make all of your phone calls at once, and pre-schedule any personal meetings on your list that you may have been putting off. Or decide you've been putting them off for a good reason, and just take them off the list.

Other questions that may help you prioritize your list:

• Is everything on the list important? You can give some items an X priority (so they filter down to the bottom of the list when you sort by priority) if you want to keep them on the list, but at least temporarily move them 'off the table' so to speak. I use Z priority to keep something on the list that's been completed, but I might want to remember or reuse the item description later.

- Must all of the items be done by you personally?

- Is there a way you can automate any of these tasks, or get help with some of the tedious aspects not directly related to client contact?

- If you're not good at client contact or something else required to complete a task, or if you get a sinking feeling whenever you look at something on the list, is there someone you trust who can help you, or can you get some training to improve your skills?

This is a good time to consider what Marshall Goldsmith tells his clients to ask themselves:

> "What am I willing to change now? Not in a few months. Not when I get caught up. Now. Then get started on the activity within two weeks, or take it off the list. And quit tormenting yourself!" – Marshall Goldsmith

It's a Working Document

The list can and should change over time. Because it becomes a working list, it's important to back it up. I keep a budget for my money in Excel, and I do a [File, Save As] occasionally with the current month and year so I have a backup. The same principle applies when budgeting time and resources. It's a valuable list of chosen responsibilities and promises. It's important to have a backup copy.

Note: If the items in your Excel spreadsheet become very complicated with many dependencies (meaning: when one item can't be started until another is completed), you may wish to use Microsoft Project for these larger projects.

Clear Your Desk

You may have made your Excel list just from your memory. Now I want you to go through physical things cluttering your work area and add them to your list. You'll then have two records of the project or item: one on your Excel list, and one in your pseudo-list ... the floating pieces of paper meant to remind you some day. You can probably toss the scrap of paper.

Before you start disentangling the assorted items on your desk, create places to put the items as you find them, so you can sort as you're exploring.

If you have file folders, make a file folder for each such as: Now, Soon, Someday, File, Research and any other categories you think are important. You may want a separate folder for major projects you're involved with or contemplating, or certain people you're responsible to or for.

If you don't have file folders, clear a space on the floor and put each word in large letters (with a bold marker if you have one handy) on separate pieces of paper, and place the papers on the floor so you have room to see the category while you place the items you find next to the category names.

If you have boxes or baskets or plastic tubs you can use to keep the items sorted for future reference, place them next to the category names now.

Sort the Papers

Try to do this quickly without getting bogged down in any business you find to do, unless you only have ten minutes to get your tax return to the post office or pick up your child ... I understand!

Otherwise, try to stick to this task and just get through it. Pick up one piece of paper at a time, quickly determine which pile it goes into, and put it there. Keep going until every nook and cranny of your working space is clear of clutter.

Enjoy Some Freedom!

Don't look at the content of the piles yet. Just look at your space and enjoy the feeling of freedom! You've just cleared your work space!

Find the appropriate cleaning products and wipe down the surface of your desk or work area. Polish it if it's wood. Dust the space around your desk.

Take a step back and look at your work space. Start a shopping list for items that can make your work space more fun to be around.

Is your chair comfortable? Do you need any padding or support on the seat, behind your lumbar area, under your feet, to be really comfortable there?

How is the lighting? Can you see what's on your desk at all times of day or night? Is the intensity and quality of the light pleasant and inviting?

Look at each item in your work area. Does it have a purpose? Will it help you complete your work and help you feel supported? Does it give you a good feeling? Move anything you don't need, or that doesn't feel wonderful or helpful to you, to a pile near the door.

Look at your work area again. Is there anything missing? Make another list of things to add to your work space: photos of people or places important to you, a picture that represents your goal, office supplies or tools you've missed as you've tried to do your work here before.

When you're satisfied that you have a clear plan to create a wonderful work space for yourself, give yourself a pat on the back and start putting things away.

Move the pile of things near the door to the garage or another holding place for review later. Put the piles of paper somewhere near your work space where you can get to them easily, but they don't clutter your wonderful new work area.

Vacuum or sweep the floor, then go shopping for the items on your list.

While you're out shopping, let your mind wander to what you love. Think about what matters to you in life, and what you'd do if you had all the resources in the world at your disposal. What really makes you happy? When you get home, write down any ideas you had that could be seeds or clues to living your life more fully … if only you had more time, energy, money, opportunity, etc. Put this paper somewhere safe that you can refer to during your Focus Session (page 28).

What to do with the piles of paper you've just created? Schedule a time to go through one pile at a time.

Find Your Direction

You may already know exactly what your goals are, and you may have defined your mission perfectly. If so, please consider this an opportunity to revisit your assumptions. You may confirm you're exactly on track, or you may discover some aspects of your life, the project, your values, that can help you update portions of your existing plan.

You'll be working with this more in the next chapter "Values to Daily Tasks". What I want you to do now is document what you already know, what you're carrying around in your head that may or may not have been examined in awhile.

Wellness and Vitality

Are you operating at your best? Have you taken good care of the most essential engine that runs you and your business (your body)? Are you getting good nutrition, drinking enough water, getting exercise and enough sleep? Add important tasks that support your health to your Excel spreadsheet as needed.

Your Goals

You now have a list of tasks. Let's make a list of goals you've taken on.

- What goals do you have day to day?

- What projects have you agreed to take on? What role do you play, or what part of the project are you responsible for?

- Do you have goals for your health?

- For your social life?

- For your family?

- For your spiritual life?

- For your charity?

26

- For your finances?

- For your home?

Write them all down. You don't have to prioritize yet; just make a list for later reference.

Social Media Mission or Purpose

You'll be working with these ideas again in the next chapter "Values to Daily Tasks", but again for now, I just want you to document the working premise you're currently using for your life. You may or may not want to change anything; it's just helpful to have it in writing where you can see it more objectively.

What is your purpose in business or your personal life that leads you to investing time and money in social media?

How would you describe the successful outcome of your social media campaign? Be as specific as you can. It's okay if this changes; it's just helpful to have a clear idea of where you're starting.

What are the reasons you've chosen the goals above? Write down some words or phrases next to each that describe those reasons.

Do you notice any patterns? Write down sentences that describe patterns, that also resonate with you as reflecting your mission or purpose.

Follow Up

In the next chapter we'll be looking at values and daily tasks, so you'll have a better idea of what to focus on then. While we're talking about time management, I'll take the opportunity to suggest some ways to structure your day.

Attitude

How do you begin and end your day? Consider beginning the day waking up in happy anticipation of the inventive ways Life will bring new and wonderful things to you today. And consider ending your day by reviewing what happened with gratitude and appreciation, forgiving yourself and others for any blunders and absurdities. Sometimes feelings are a choice. We can choose gratitude and curiosity rather than a host of more negative feelings. How does attitude fit into a time management chapter? We make better decisions and see more opportunities and resources when we're thinking about what could work, rather than what's wrong and who's to blame.

Focus Session

Part of my routine every day includes what I call a Focus Session. I keep hearing how important focus is to people who have become very successful, and I find this so useful myself that I offer it to you as another tool to keep yourself on track. It's a great way to start the day before everyone else's priorities eclipse your own. Here's my recipe:

- I sit down in a quiet place with my planner and look at my values and goals, and allow myself to feel what I will experience when I actually achieve those goals.

- Then I look at what I have planned for the upcoming day, and see how closely they are aligned with my values and overall goals.

- Is everything I'm planning to do actually addressing my needs, or have I taken on responsibilities that are not mine?

- What can I add to my day to inspire and keep me happy?

28

All of this takes about five minutes. I do this again throughout the day as I have time.

Systems

Do you use a planner or PDA, or are you operating from floating pieces of paper that seem to get lost regularly? Are you keeping track of your promises or are meetings and commitments falling through the cracks? When you start your day, do you know what you expect from yourself?

You now have a master Excel spreadsheet of commitments and plans. Let's explore how you would put a task into a planner, and keep track of important information as you go throughout your day.

Use Your Planner

An easy, free way to keep track of your calendar: download Palm Desktop, which you can use even if you don't have a PDA. Alternatively use Outlook or software that comes with your PDA if you track things digitally. Keeping track on paper in an old-fashioned dependable planner also works! By the way, if my instructions don't match exactly with how your planner or PDA works, just look on your device for a function similar to what I describe.

Tasks Related to Time

Some tasks, like meeting someone for lunch or attending a staff meeting, have a relationship with a specific time. That's easy: Find the date and time in your planner, and enter the event there. Be sure to include contact name and phone number, along with the name and address of restaurant or venue if the event is outside your office.

Other tasks related to time may happen every week, like your weekly study group or poker game. Some tasks or events occur every weekday like going to work, some every month like getting a paycheck, and some every year like your birthday.

Some tasks aren't related to time at all. Maybe it's your honey-do list on the refrigerator, or your wish list of things to buy or places to visit.

Choose a quiet time each day and schedule 15 minutes for your Focus Session (page page 28). This will probably only take five minutes, but in case you want more time one day, I suggest scheduling 15 minutes. If you don't need it, you can start your day feeling like you're ahead of time instead of feeling like you're starting from behind.

You'll soon be adding your social media routine to your schedule. As you look at your schedule, seeif you can fine 10 minutes or one hour time periods to test the social media waters.

How do you keep track of these easily?

Add Recurring Tasks

Start by adding non-negotiable time commitments like going to work. If this happens on a regular schedule, for instance 9a-5p Monday-Friday, first create a task for the first day, Monday. Set the start time as 9:00 a.m. and end time as 5:00 p.m. Find the button that allows you to make this a recurring task and select Daily, then either weekdays or Monday, Tuesday, Wednesday, Thursday and Friday. If this is an ongoing arrangement select No End Date.

Master Task List

For tasks that occur at a specific time, enter them at the appropriate time in your calendar.

For tasks without a specific time, enter them into a master task list. This is a list that resides somewhere outside of your calendar, but within your planner program. The list follows you every day, allows you to check off items as they're completed, and optimally can be sorted by priority or category. This may end up being an Excel spreadsheet, but it's easier to keep everything together in one application, because having only one thing to carry around or remember makes it simpler to track and back up data.

Updates Throughout the Day

Carry around some mechanism to help you keep a record of what occurs during the day. This might be your PDA if you type really fast on those tiny keyboards, it might be your paper planner, or it could just be a small notebook. This is where you'll take notes at the meetings you attend, including details about the next meeting and your deliverables. Suggested format:

Name of Meeting
Names of people attending
Notes about meeting
Notes and dates of your deliverables

Or notes about an upcoming meeting:

Name of Upcoming Meeting – Date and time of meeting
Name and address of venue
Notes about meeting
Notes about your deliverables for meeting

Or notes about referrals:

Name of Referral – by Name of Person Referring
Contact information
Information about the person and situation or needs
Whether the person referring will introduce you
When and how to follow up with the referral and the person
referring (Note: Add this as a task in your Master Task List of at
the appointed time in your calendar.)

Summary

- Make a list of everything you can think of you're responsible to carry out.

- Look at the purpose of each item, and who you're doing this for.

- Is everything on the list important?

- Must all of the items be accomplished by you personally?

- Is there someone you trust who can help you?

- Would any sort of training help you take care of certain items?

- Clear your desk and sort the papers.

- Make your work space pleasant to support your work easily.

- Have you added tasks to take care of your health and vitality?

- Make a list of goals you've taken on.

- Describe how you envision the successful outcome of your social media campaign.

- Include a Focus Session (page 28) as part of your day.

- Convert any floating pieces of paper into entries in your planner or PDA.

- As you go through the day, write your notes in your planner or PDA to record important information and commitments.

CHAPTER 4

Values to Daily Tasks

&

We get so busy in our lives doing what we're supposed to do, carrying out tasks handed out by someone else, that it's easy to lose track of our own values in terms of our goals. The more distance between what matters to us and our daily tasks as we spend our precious time, the more likely we are to become tired and discouraged, and the more likely to lose focus, burn out and forget why we're doing our work.

Happiness comes from following through on what matters to you, so if you're checking off tasks throughout the day that you know build on what you care about, it'll go a long way toward increasing your enjoyment of your day. Your authentic level of happiness comes through as you talk with clients and prospective partners. People are attracted to sincere happiness and confidence.

Identifying Values

How do you even know what your values are? I borrow some questions from the noted psychologist Nathaniel Branden, from his book *The Art of Living Consciously* (Simon & Schuster ISBN: 978-0-684-81084-3), where you'll find his entire program.

I've seen Marshall Goldsmith use one of these questions in a group setting. As everyone sits in a circle, each person asks themselves the same question and answers the question in turn, going around the circle several times. What happens is the first answer comes from the surface, with each subsequent answer going a bit deeper, then finally getting to the core of what really matters to each participant.

Take notes as you think through your answers. Choose only one question at a time.

I respect people most when they …
One of the principles that guides me is …
One of the things I want out of life is …
One of the things I want from people is …
One of the things I want from work is …
One of the things I expect of myself is …
I am becoming aware …
Life seems most fulfilling when …
Life seems most painful when …

Ranking

Now that you have your list of values, rank them in order of importance to you.

Start with your most important value. Think about how the outcome of that value could manifest in your life by this time next year. Write a clear description of this, including how you will feel as you experience this positive outcome of what matters most to you, and let yourself express those feelings now. Make it about you and your experience, not about someone else's life.

• When you have the description, think about when, realistically, this might actually happen.

• Now make a list of the practical steps it would take to bring this about.

• Break them down into what has to happen monthly and weekly to make this happen.

Daily Tasks

Pull out your planner:

• Put your list of values and goals on a separate page in your planner where you can refer to it during your Focus Session.

• Put these goals into your planner by month and week as appropriate.

• Now think about some task you can do every day to get closer to this goal.

• Put this task, or these tasks, on your daily pages, or a master task list that you look at every day.

Review

Compare what you've discovered in this chapter with the lists you created in Chapter 4. Make priority and other changes in your Master Task List to more effectively support your core values.

Summary

• Define what really matters to you.

• Rank your list of values in order of importance to you.

• Make a list of practical steps to manifest your values in your life.

• Add these to your planner by monthly, weekly and daily tasks as appropriate.

CHAPTER 5

Automating and Delegating

ဆာ

This can all be very time consuming. Many of these tasks (like tweets) are very personal to you. Other tasks can be delegated to some trusted person who understands your style, your point of view and your business. Still other tasks can be automated as social media tools increasingly allow you to connect your various accounts together.

As I write this chapter I'm trying to keep it very, very basic. I also see that even the basics make a somewhat long and involved chapter. Please remember to just take what you like and can use for now, and leave the rest. Even if you only implement one part of one step, you'll gain some benefit as long as you approach this effort aligned with the image you want to convey online, and you keep in mind your overall focus for your business and your life.

What You Need to Keep

Social media is about people connecting with people, not people broadcasting their message for a one-way conversation, or for organizations disseminating their sanitized message to the masses. This means if you're going to have a social media presence it needs to be about a person. If you are the main brand of your small business, then the face and voice needs to be yours personally.

Companies whose brand is not a specific person have found success in designating one spokesperson. For instance, Scott Monty is the voice of Ford Motor Company on Ford's Twitter account. This way Ford has a consistent voice on Twitter, and people who want to connect with Ford or communicate with Ford know they're actually connecting with a real person.

If you are your company's brand but you don't have time to keep up the account personally, you may ask someone who is very familiar with you and your business, who understands your voice, to help you. In this case it's a good idea to be clear with your followers there are two of you tweeting, for instance. I've worked with Marshall Goldsmith for several years with his online presence, and he's asked me to work with his social media accounts. We make an effort to be very clear to anyone following him who is speaking when we send a tweet. Transparency and authenticity are very important to build credibility and connection with your audience.

Beyond your face and your voice, when you think about actually sitting with your computer or mobile device to send updates and keep up with your accounts, and you consider what specific tasks to keep and to delegate, instead of thinking of this whole thing as one more project to add to your already overflowing schedule, think first about the overall function of your job and how the areas of people contact (with customers, vendors, the public in general) and market research fit into your role.

Twitter is the most dynamic, real-time free market research tool available. You can ask your assistant to provide you with daily reports of trends, and maybe that's enough. Or maybe you'll get more value from watching the actual conversations as they happen.

I'm not trying to sell you on opening up your schedule to another big time commitment. I'm just asking you to look at what you're doing now, and think about how social media might be able to streamline the way you're doing things already and put you in a position of being on top of your stakeholders' current thoughts and activities. Trying a new way of managing old tasks could prove very interesting and useful.

Blog

How often do you find yourself giving the very same update to a new person? If the update is something you'd like to be known publicly, why not write a blog post for all the world to see? You can verbally tell people about the topic, and then direct them to this blog post or page for specifics.

Do you want your stakeholders, customers, staff to keep in mind your organization's point of view, mission statement, or refer to a list of contacts or resources? Putting them where everyone can easily reference them could be useful … if it's also a message you want out in the public. If not, you may consider adding a blog function to your company intranet.

LinkedIn

Would you find it useful to send a message to your entire professional network all at once? Would you like to stay on top of what your colleagues are up to?

LinkedIn doesn't have to take a lot of your time, and if you're a professional that depends on your professional network, it can be a great time-saver and expand your reach exponentially.

It's also a great way to keep current with address and employment changes … to let others know about changes in your life, and to maintain up-to-date information about your colleagues.

Facebook

If your Facebook profile is used primarily for close family and friends, you can create privacy settings and only friend the people you want to see your most intimate information. With the right privacy settings it can be a great way to share photos, information and updates with people close to you.

If you prefer a more open approach, you can use Facebook to find old friends and contacts through the search engine on Facebook, and through Facebook's Friend Finder.

Twitter

Track real-time updates about your market and on the news by either going to search.twitter.com and searching on your key search terms (your company name, keywords for your industry, your name, etc.), or setting up these searches in a third-party application (go to Google, Bing or Yahoo and search for 'twitter keyword alert' to find available applications).

Help From the Internet

There are more online services available than I've been able to count. I keep a list of new sites and services I find that look useful, and the list just keeps growing. I'll present a few specifics in this chapter, with more in Volume 4 of this series *Social Media Strategy*. If you need something slightly different than I suggest, just go to one of the major search engines like Google, Yahoo or Bing and do a search for what you want. You can also sometimes find comparisons by typing in more than one name of the services into one search. For instance, if you type 'WordPress Drupal Joomla' you'll probably find a comparison chart of those three software programs. I say 'probably' because by the time you read this things might have changed.

When you come across something you don't understand, search engines are your friend. What do my web developer friends do when they come across an error message while they're developing software, or my computer hardware friends when they're troubleshooting a computer issue? They copy the error message they see on the screen, and they paste it verbatim into a search engine, and voila! Up comes a list of other people's comments who have had the exact same issue.

Use this concept as you find yourself in unfamiliar territory. Adding the word 'tutorial' to a technical word is another trick I use to find people who have generously shared their knowledge about a particular technical task. Well, sometimes they've done this so they can post their ads which they hope you'll click on so they make some money. You can usually weave your way around the ads to find the content and learn what you needed to understand. To find the definition of a new technical term, just type in 'definition' and the new word.

Blog

Publishing a blog post means it's going out to the world and potentially could be listed by search engines. This can be even more effective than a traditional press release.

There is often a section on blog software for a 'blogroll', or a list of other people's blogs that you find relevant and want to share with your blog visitors. Add blogs there you want to follow yourself (making it easier for you to find them) or add blogs strategically that will help you with your customers or stakeholders (also saving you the time of hunting for this in front of your customer).

Use keywords in your blog posts that are related to what you do, what you want to be known for, and what search terms your key potential customers are currently using. You can learn more about this in Volume 1 *Social Media for Beginners* and for more advanced information, Volume 4 *Social Media Strategy.* For now just choose some terms you think are important and add them within context to the text of your posts.

LinkedIn

If you're looking for a new expert or someone to introduce you to the right person in a new company, check your connections in LinkedIn, and look into their connections.

Expand your reach in terms of being seen as an expert by interacting in the Answers area.

Facebook

You can use Facebook as a research tool in two ways:

Sign into your Facebook account and use the search box there to find people, pages and groups within Facebook that match what you're looking for, or that may lead you to what you're looking for.

Go to Google, Bing or Yahoo and type in your search term with the word 'Facebook' at the end to find references available to the general public (people who are not members of Facebook).

Twitter

You'll be surprised at what you can learn and who you can meet quickly and personally by interacting on Twitter.

Go to search.twitter.com to find real-time and very recent posts by searching on your key search terms, your company name, your name, your Twitter handle @marilynmcleod.

Help From Your Focus

I can't say enough about the importance of knowing exactly what you want. This saves everyone so much time, especially you. There are times it's best not to have an unshakable linear focus, so we can learn and adjust our course as we go forward and the environment changes. There are also times to point the way and just plain get to the destination. If you choose a less rigid approach, just be sure to know exactly what you want, so you can refer back to where you started and your original purpose when things get confusing.

It's great to make course corrections. It's not so useful to just drift about … unless that's your style and it's working very well for you. If this is your style you'll probably need some more grounded, linear people around you to make any forward progress … if indeed you want to make some forward progress. Life isn't always about accomplishment. Sometimes it's just about exploring, learning, and enjoying.

Blog

Create an editorial calendar with topics that support your activities throughout the year.

Create an About page that you can show people when you're introducing them to your company. This will save you time explaining details, and give people a reference point for follow up later.

LinkedIn

Make strategic updates to let your network know of your activities and accomplishments.

Ask and answer questions strategically in the Answers section. This many help you find new opportunities or strengthen relationships with people in your network.

Facebook

To convey your focus and point of view online, as a business I recommend a Facebook Fan Page rather than a profile, which I describe in Volume 4 *Social Media Strategy.*

Twitter

Create a custom background that clearly conveys your desired image and message.

Make sure your web link goes directly to the most informative web page you have that describes your desired image and message.

Tweet from your point of view with a message style that's consistent with the rest of your online marketing. Twitter is more personal but as a business you want to remember to maintain a respectful, professional tone. Maybe a good analogy is 'business casual'!

Help From Your Systems

Do you have systems you use in your work now? Do you always have staff meetings on Monday mornings and always call your spouse at lunch to check in? Do you meet with your assistant at the end of the day to catch up on loose ends, or meet the gang after work before going home?

What's working for you now? What's getting in the way of your focus? What are you missing? Where could you use more support, more information, more resources?

Take a step back and see if you can make adjustments to your existing systems to increase efficiency, effectiveness, and enjoyment of your day.

From that point of view, what could be automated that you're already doing? What could be delegated to either free up your personal time or your staff's personal time? Is someone else better qualified to handle any of these tasks? What would you like to get off your plate? Could that be automated or delegated?

Blog

Create a page for each type of information you and your staff find yourselves providing to people over and over again. Answer these frequently asked questions online in one place where everyone can find them.

When you and your staff hear questions from your customers and stakeholders that you think important to clarify or highlight, write a blog post about it.

LinkedIn

Continually expand your personal network by sending LinkedIn invitations to people who have agreed to connect with you on LinkedIn (be sure to use the address you're using on LinkedIn or you'll end up with stray LinkedIn accounts), and accept invitations from people you want in your personal network.

Monitor the LinkedIn email updates and note changes to contact information for your key connections.

Download your LinkedIn contacts regularly to an Excel or .csv file. If someone disconnects from you all of their information is deleted, so a backup is important.

Facebook

Facebook profile functionality is limited, so I recommend a Facebook Fan Page if you're wanting more functionality to help you with your office systems. See Volume 4 *Social Media Strategy* for more information.

Twitter

Use Twitter to gain insight into your part of the marketplace.

When you look at the list of people who have chosen to follow you, what do you think their purpose is in choosing to follow you? What do you think they want? Is this something you want to provide? Is this an indication of a new direction you or your company may want to go?

Create 120 character posts of information you want to convey to people who may be listening. Intersperse your self-serving messages between messages highlighting other people and their ideas.

Help from Online Automation

The first step in automation is to add your photo (a professional head shot) to gravatar.com. Many sites pull your photo from gravatar.com, so if you use a consistent email address as you move around the web, commenting on blogs and joining sites, you can have a consistent image and save a lot of time by registering with gravatar.com.

OpenID is another time-saver, as well as security measure. Some sites allow you to register using your OpenID account instead of using your private password and information each time you register for a new site.

PayPal offers a similar service in terms of giving out credit card and financial information. It's an inexpensive way to receive credit card payments and build a shopping cart just by using their html code which you can develop yourself on their website. You'll just need to know where to insert the html into your web page. Your web developer can help with that, or even perhaps your web designer.

The first strategic move I recommend: create alerts on your search terms to receive an email when your search term is mentioned online. Some key services available: Twilert, Tweetbeep andGoogle alerts.

Another helpful service is url shorteners. Using this service gives you two benefits:

The obvious benefit is a shorter url. This is especially helpful in emails and Twitter, and especially when you have a very long url.

If the url shortener site also provides tracking, you can actually watch how many people are clicking on your link just as you would with Google Analytics.

Blog

You can extend your blog's reach by sending your blog's RSS feed through other online services. RSS is a technical terms that you don't need to understand in order to use it. Just find the RSS feed link for your blog (you can probably find this in the settings panel of your blog software), and copy it into a text file you save in your RESOURCES folder (discussed in Volume 1 Social Media for Beginners) for handy reference later. It's just a special url that takes people to the raw file of all blogs you've posted instead of the pretty interface you see when you go to your main blog site.

Create a Feedburner account and add your blog (you'll need to know your RSS feed url for this). Then find the Feedburner link and paste that into the 'subscribe to this blog' feature in your blog software. That'll send people to Feedburner's free subscription service, and you'll be able to keep track of statistics (not names of people) about who's receiving your blog feed.

There are also services like PostLater which allow you to prepare blog posts in advance and preschedule them for publication later. This can be a good strategy for content posts about topics that aren't likely to change or be politically insensitive depending on current events. Use this as an adjunct to posts you write as you respond to current events and make your own special announcements.

LinkedIn

Copy your blog's RSS feed url to the blog application in LinkedIn so your blog posts display automatically in your LinkedIn profile.

Facebook

Copy your blog's RSS feed url to the Notes tab (click on the Notes tab and look on the right side of the page for the 'edit' link) so your blog posts display automatically in your Facebook profile.

Twitter

Feedburner allows you to send your blog feed directly into your Twitter account by adding your Twitter login to your Feedburner account. This allows your blog posts to display automatically in your Twitter stream.

You can preschedule tweets with applications like TweetLater, Hootsuite and SocialOomph. As with blog posts, this can be a good strategy for content posts about topics that aren't likely to change or be politically insensitive depending on current events. You can use this as an adjunct to tweets you send to respond to current events and announcements you want to make.

Review

A diagram of the ecosystem I've described above may be helpful. Please note all of these functions are optional. To preschedule:

Blog posts: PostLater => Blog => Feedburner => Twitter

Twitter posts: TweetLater => Twitter

To post real time simply go to the website and login, then send a status update:

> Blog
> LinkedIn
> Facebook
> Twitter

To extend your blog's reach copy your blog's RSS feed url to:

> LinkedIn (blog section of your profile)
> Facebook (notes tab in your profile)
> Twitter (from your Feedburner account)

You can see from the above that your message can travel online very quickly, especially when you take into consideration all of the people subscribing to Google alerts and Twitter alerts using the keywords you're highlighting in your posts. This can be very helpful or very unhelpful, depending on the content and timing of your post.

If you've prescheduled a post that highlights you as a rich millionaire because of your association with a pre-eminent company and you suddenly get a Google alert that tells you the company is under investigation for tax evasion, go into your prescheduling service and don't send that post just yet. Or rewrite it to make your point in a different way.

This week when I was in my LinkedIn account I noticed a status update from a young man touting a new drinking game with a link to a video on some site I didn't recognize. I wondered how potential employers would view that post, and I wondered if he wrote that post in a personal niche networking account somewhere and then forgot he'd added the feed to his LinkedIn account.

I'll remind you again ... be careful what you post. Be sure you know the image and message you want to convey online, and try to stay on message. I'm not saying don't interact in a personal way, and I'm definitely not suggesting you stick to your sanitized message. That's not what social media and social networking is about. I am saying think before you post ... would your spouse, mother, children, or potential employer or client trust you more or less for what you're about to say? If you've been drinking or are otherwise disconnected from your critical mind, make a note to yourself about what you want to say, and write the post later when you're fully conscious and aware again.

Help From Your Peers

There are ways you and your colleagues can help each other online. I'll describe this from your point of view; remember you can do the same for your colleagues.

Blog

Think of the image you want to convey online, and how your blog will help support that message. Think of people you know whose contribution you value that would also support your message, and are people who will not compete with what you're selling to your target audience. Ask them to become guest bloggers on your blog, or to contribute an article here and there. Offer to give them a link back to their website within their blog post.

Ask them to add a link to your blog on their website or to the blogroll on their blog.

LinkedIn

Watch for opportunities as you read status updates from your colleagues.

Ask for their help when you need information or resources they may have access to or own.

Create a poll to help you make a decision or take the next step in designing your new program or product.

Facebook

If you're using your Facebook profile account in a public way (which is still available only to people with Facebook accounts who are logged in), you can send a status update or message your friends via email and ask for something or provide helpful information.

Twitter

Think of who you'd like to have following you to receive your updates, and cultivate those relationships. Find their Twitter account and follow them. Give them credit within Twitter by retweeting their interesting messages to your followers, including their Twitter handle (@marilynmcleod for instance) in your retweeted message. Thank them publicly as appropriate.

I've heard of people tweeting to ask for help when they're traveling and receiving some valuable local assistance.

Also of people traveling who suddenly have time on their hands and are able to meet one of their local followers in person for coffee.

If you see breaking news your followers would appreciate, announce it through a tweet.

Follow important people in your industry and read their tweets. Respond to them, retweet with attribution, and interact with them to build trust and rapport.

Help From Support Staff

One key task someone can help you with is to monitor your online reputation and do real-time research of activity that matters to you. They can also look for new people for you to connect with, or find contact information for people you've met or been associated with in the past that you'd like to add to your current network. You can ask your staff to provide you with regular reports of what they find.

- Monitor alerts on keywords related to you and your business (Google alerts and Twilert)

- Track mentions of your company, brand, products, services, competitors, etc.

- Real-time research on search.twitter.com.

- Search directories like Twellow to find people in your ideal audience.

- Send and monitor polls.

One scenario might look this way:

- You ask Person A to track and monitor your brand and mentions of your company and your product, positive and negative.

- Person A forwards the messages they find to Person B in your company who knows that part of your company inside and out. Person B responds immediately to the tweet, or makse a comment on the blog post.

- Person B monitors online response to their comments or tweet, and looks for indications of the market changing, or new opportunities in the marketplace.

Think of any negative messages more than as just complaints to deal with. Consider them an early warning system for your organization, look for trends, and consider how your organization can adapt to address your customers' concerns and perceptions.

By the same token, it's just as important to respond to people who say positive things about your brand as it is to respond to those who complain or point out errors.

A related point which I've learned from online application developers: Instead of building out your entire widget with all the bells and whistles you're sure your ideal customers need and want, get something started and then ask them what they want. Listen to them as they use and interact with your widget. Add the bells and whistles they actually need. Interact with them and give them a voice in how your widget develops. The end product will probably surprise you, and it'll cost fewer resources to develop.

Blog

If you're not a writer you can ask someone else to draft posts for you. In order to maintain your voice, it's best for you to do the final editing before they're posted.

If you enjoy writing but can't spell and get the grammar all mixed up, you might want to do the writing yourself and have someone else proof and post for you. Unless you trust them completely, you may want to review the final before it's posted publicly.

LinkedIn

Someone else can download your contacts as a backup.

They can also monitor the LinkedIn updates email that comes through, and update any contact information changes in the software you use to keep track of your contacts.

Someone else can add your blog RSS feed to your LinkedIn profile.

Facebook

Someone else can do searches for Facebook accounts, groups and fan pages about a topic of interest to you.

They can also schedule events, place ads, and add your blog RSS feed in the Notes tab.

Twitter

You can hand someone a list of search terms and ask them to summarize what they find on search.twitter.com.

You can ask someone to set up alerts for you on Twilert or Tweetbeep.

Summary

• Instead of viewing your social media efforts as one more big time commitment, look instead for ways social media could streamline tasks already taking up time in your schedule.

• What can you delegate? Can you have someone ghostwrite for you in your voice? You can have someone on your team tracking and monitoring your brand and online conversations, and moderating your fan page or group.

• You think Twitter takes a lot of time and you want someone else to tweet for you. Do you really know someone you can trust to respond as you would, with your words, with your point of view, to support your goals and your message? Do they really know you and your company that well? And will you know what "you" just tweeted if you're at a meeting and someone in the audience sees a tweet coming through from you on their PDA and makes a comment to you about it on the spot? If you have someone else tweeting for you, give them a face and have them put their initials on their tweets.

• Just remember what you're after is rapport and trust from your audience. Lack of authenticity does come through, so it's better to have fewer tweets and have them authentic, than to have lots of tweets that lower trust with your audience. You are the one with the personal touch and it's your voice.

CHAPTER 6

Universal Needs Chart

ℰↄ

Why do I have this weird section about needs in a time management book? Quite simply because I've found this concept can save a tremendous amount of time when dealing with people, most especially with myself.

How it Works

Everyone has feelings and needs which propel them into behaviors, conclusions, choices and messages that may or may not be the best strategies to meet their needs. Most people are not conscious of which of their needs are driving them, or why they're so unhappy or unfulfilled.

Most people who react to the behaviors, conclusions, choices and messages of the people around them are also not aware of the person's needs, or their own needs as they react within their own habitual patterns.

We can spend countless hours, years and decades going around in circles explaining why it's someone else's fault, telling our same sad stories, railing against the same seemingly insurmountable conditions. The people around us can spend those same countless hours and decades debating the pros and cons with us, telling us why we shouldn't be so upset, arguing why they're not to blame and making their explanations.

Why doesn't this work? Because nobody has figured out what they really need. They're all arguing about strategies, having conflicts with what they perceive as 'the enemy'. The odd and amazing truth at the bottom of it all ... we all have the same needs. Often people locked into the most difficult conflicts share exactly the same basic, universal needs. If they can get past their stories and enemy images and actually open their hearts to hear the human being they've locked horns with, chances are each party will discover they're both fighting for safety or recognition or significance or some other universal need. When they can both recognize this and drop the rest, it's also amazing how quickly they can agree on a strategy that will work for both of them.

What does this have to do with social media and time management?

I think it's useful to shortcut the chatter and drama and be able to identify, or at least make a heartfelt guess, as to the need someone we're dealing with might be trying to meet. Then hopefully instead of becoming embroiled in the hopeless mental landscape they've invited us into, we can come from a different place and have a more productive conversation for both of us.

It's also useful to be aware of our own needs so we can make our own choices based on meeting those needs. We'll be happier and healthier, and we'll spend much less time dithering and squander fewer resources on things that on the surface seem like they'll give us the safety, recognition or significance we're looking for, but actually just end up helping us feel a bit lonelier and more empty.

I include this list of needs because it's a useful reference when identifying the reason behind someone's behavior we don't understand, or our own feelings. When we can identify the need, we're very close to mediating conflicts, finding a solution that will work, or moving closer to a very fulfilling life.

How to Use the Chart

The following list of needs is neither exhaustive nor definitive. It is meant as a starting place to support anyone who wishes to engage in a process of deepening self-discovery and to facilitate greater understanding and connection between people.

For more information read *Conscious Networking* by Marilyn McLeod. For now, just use this list as a guide when trying to identify someone's underlying need to help you relate to them in a significant way.

Connection
acceptance
affection
appreciation
belonging
cooperation
communication
closeness
community
companionship
compassion
consideration
consistency
empathy
inclusion
intimacy
love
mutuality
nurturing
respect/self-respect
safety
security
stability

support
to know and be known
to see and be seen
to understand and
be understood
trust
warmth

Physical Wellbeing
air
food
movement/exercise
rest/sleep
sexual expression
safety
shelter
touch
water

Honesty
authenticity
integrity
presence

Play
joy
humor

Peace
beauty
communion
ease
equality
harmony
inspiration
order

Meaning
awareness
celebration of life
challenge
clarity
competence
consciousness
contribution
creativity
discovery
efficacy
effectiveness
growth
hope
learning
mourning
participation
purpose
self-expression
stimulation
to matter
understanding

Autonomy
choice
freedom
independence
space
spontaneity

Needs Chart (c) 2005 by Center for Nonviolent Communication
Website: www.cnvc.org Email: cnvc@cnvc.org
Phone: +1.505-244-4041

CHAPTER 7

Follow Up

ဆ

How are you feeling now about fitting some aspect of social media into your busy schedule? I hope you've found a few ways to streamline work you're doing now and I hope you'll discover ways that social media can actually save time while expanding your reach. I hope you enjoy and benefit from tapping into the real-time conversation in your area of the marketplace.

You'll have questions as you continue to explore this territory, and the territory will change when you're not looking! Feel free to send me a message anytime, or check online for updates.

My online hub: http://www.CoachMarilyn.com
My email: Marilyn@CoachMarilyn.com

Check http://www.CoachMarilyn.com for updated resources as social media and the Internet evolve and I learn more. Add what you've learned!

Join the conversation with me and watch for updates

http://www.Twitter.com/marilynmcleod
http://www.Facebook.com/7Steps
http://www.LinkedIn.com/in/coachmarilyn

Contact me!

I'd love to hear from you! Please let me know how this book is working for you, and check with the readers group with questions and to add new information you find!

Marilyn McLeod
Marilyn@CoachMarilyn.com
San Diego 2010